POPCORN RECIPES

Table of Contents

1) **Brown Butter &Parmesan Popcorn**

Preparation Time: 5 minutes
Cooking Time: 10 minutes
Ready In: 15 minutes
Servings: 4 cups

INGREDIENTS:

1/2 cup unsalted corn kernels
3 tablespoons Parmesan, grated
3 tablespoons unsalted butter
Kosher salt as per taste

DIRECTIONS:

1.
Pop the corn in microwave or in a deep pan coated with butter/vegetable oil over heat (do not use olive oil for popping the corn). The pan should be covered with a lid and remove the pan from stove only when popping slows down or pan is full. Remove any un-popped kernels.

2.
Place a small pan over medium heat and melt the butter in it. Use a wooden spoon to stir it while melting till it starts to foam. Do this for about a minute. This should turn the butter into golden brown color and smell nutty.

3.
Add the parmesan and salt to the melted butter. (If the butter starts to solidify by this time, heat it again to re-melt).

4.
Pour the melted butter and parmesan mix over the popcorn and toss well. Enjoy!

2) Popcorn with Caramel

Preparation Time: 15 minutes
Cooking Time: 50 minutes
Ready In: 1 hour and 5 minutes
Servings: 4 cups

INGREDIENTS:

1/2cupunsalted cornkernels
1/2 cup Light or Dark corn syrup
1/2 teaspoon baking soda
1 cup brown sugar
1/2 cup butter
1 teaspoon Pure Vanilla Extract
Cooking Spray
Salt as per taste

DIRECTIONS:

1.
Pop the corn in microwave or in a deep pan coated with butter/vegetable oil over heat
(do not use olive oil for popping the corn). The pan should be covered with a lid and
remove the pan from stove only when popping slows down or pan is full. Remove any
un-popped kernels.

2.
Place a small pan over medium heat and melt the butter in it. When butter melts, add
the sugar, corn syrup and salt to it and stir nicely to mix everything. Bring this mixture to
a boil.

3. Now stop stirring and boil for another 5 minutes and then remove the pan from heat.

4.
Sift in the baking soda and add the vanilla to this mix and mix nicely.

5.
Preheat an oven to 250 degrees. Line a baking dish with cooking spray.

6.

Spread the ready popcorn over this baking dish and place it in the oven for about 5 minutes just to warm the popcorn. Remove from the oven when done

7.

Pour the butter and sugar syrup over the ready popcorn and toss nicely to coat.

8.

Now again place the baking dish in the oven and bake for about 45 minutes.

9.

When done, remove from the oven and spread the popcorn on a flat surface sprinkled with cooking spray (preferably, spread them on foil paper coated with cooking spray).

10.

Let them cool. When cooled, break the caramelized popcorn into pieces and store in an air tight container or enjoy instantly!

3) Popcorn with Sesame&Ginger in Sriracha Sauce

Preparation Time: 5 minutes
Cooking Time: 10 minutes
Ready In: 15 minutes
Servings: 4 cups

INGREDIENTS:

1/2 cupunsalted corn kernels
1 tablespoon Sriracha sauce
1/2 teaspoon ginger, ground
1 1/2 teaspoon sesame seeds
2 tablespoons butter
1 teaspoon garlic powder
1 tablespoon olive oil
Salt as per taste

DIRECTIONS:

1.
Pop the corn in microwave or in a deep pan coated with butter/vegetable oil over heat (do not use olive oil for popping the corn). The pan should be covered with a lid and remove the pan from stove only when popping slows down or pan is full. Remove any un-popped kernels.

2.
Melt butter ina small pan over medium heat. When butter starts to melt, add in the olive oil and Sriracha sauce.

3.
Now mix the sesame seeds, ground ginger, garlic powder and salt to this sauce and stir nicely. The sauce should be thin in consistency.

4.
Pour this sauce over the popped popcorn and toss gently to coat well.

5.
Sprinkle some more sesame seeds on the popcorn to garnish. Enjoy!

4) Popcorn with Brown Butter, Lemon & Rosemary

Preparation Time: 5 minutes
Cooking Time: 10 minutes
Ready In: 15 minutes
Servings: 8 cups

INGREDIENTS:

1 cup unsalted corn kernels
2 tablespoonsfresh Rosemary, half finely minced and half whole leaves
4 tablespoons butter
1 tablespoon lemon zest, finely grated
Salt as per taste

DIRECTIONS:

1.
Pop the corn in microwave or in a deep pan coated with butter/vegetable oil over heat (do not use olive oil for popping the corn). The pan should be covered with a lid and remove the pan from stove only when popping slows down or pan is full. Remove any un-popped kernels.

2.
Melt butter ina small pan over medium heat. Keep heating the butter till it turns golden brown and starts to smell nutty. Keep stirring till it becomes foamy but take care not to overheat else the butter might burn.

3.
Remove the butter from heat and add rosemary, lime zest and salt to it and mix lightly. Let the mixture sit for a few seconds.

4.
Pour over the popped popcorn and toss to coat evenly.

5) Popcorn with Italian Herbs &Cheese

Preparation Time: 5 minutes
Cooking Time: 10 minutes
Ready In: 15 minutes
Servings: 8 cups

INGREDIENTS:

1 cup unsalted corn kernels
1-2 teaspoons dried Italian herbs
4 tablespoons butter
1/4 cup grated Parmesan cheese
1/2 teaspoon garlic powder
Salt and pepper as per taste

DIRECTIONS:

1.
Pop the corn in microwave or in a deep pan coated with butter/vegetable oil over heat (do not use olive oil for popping the corn). The pan should be covered with a lid and remove the pan from stove only when popping slows down or pan is full.Remove any un-popped kernels.

2.
Remove from the pan/microwave and place the popcorn on a baking dish coated with cooking spray and place in an oven at 200 degrees F to keep popcorn warm.

3.
Melt butter ina small pan over medium heat. Keep stirring with a wooden spoon.

4.
When the butter is melted, add the herbs, garlic powder, cheese, salt and pepper and mix nicely.

5. Remove popcorn from the oven and pour this mixture over them. Toss gently so thatthey are evenly coated. Divide equally among 8 cups and serve!

6) Popcorn with Roasted Peanutsin Adobo Sauce

Preparation Time: 10 minutes
Cooking Time: 25 minutes
Ready In: 35 minutes
Servings: 4 cups

INGREDIENTS:

1/2 cup unsalted corn kernels
1 tablespoon chili adobo sauce
1/4 cup peanuts
2 tablespoons sugar
1 egg white
Cooking spray
Salt and pepper as per taste

DIRECTIONS:

1.
Pop the corn in microwave or in a deep pan coated with butter/vegetable oil over heat (do not use olive oil for popping the corn). The pan should be covered with a lid and remove the pan from stove only when popping slows down or pan is full. Remove any un-popped kernels.

2.
Preheat the oven to 300 degrees F. While it is heating, prepare a large baking dish by sprinkling cooking spray on it and spread the prepared popcorn and peanuts onto it.

3.
In a small pan mix the adobo sauce, sugar, salt and egg white and whisk until the mixture becomes foamy.

4.
Pour this mixture over the popcorn and peanuts placed on the baking sheet.

5.

Bake for about 20 minutes. When done, store for later or enjoy instantly.

7) Popcorn with Pecorino Cheese &Garlic Oil

Preparation Time: 5 minutes
Cooking Time: 5 minutes
Ready In: 10minutes
Servings: 4 cups

INGREDIENTS:

1/2 cup unsalted corn kernels
1/2 cup Pecorino or Parmesan cheese, finely grated
2 garlic cloves
2 tablespoons olive oil
Salt as per taste

DIRECTIONS:

1.
Pop the corn in microwave or in a deep pan coated with butter/vegetable oil over heat (do not use olive oil for popping the corn). The pan should be covered with a lid and remove the pan from stove only when popping slows down or pan is full. Remove any un-popped kernels.

2.
In a small pan over medium heat, mix the oil and garlic cloves and heat until golden brown. When done, strain the oil by removing the garlic from it.

3.
Pour the garlic flavored oil over warm popcorn and sprinkle the cheese on it. The warm oil and popcorn will melt the cheese. Toss gently to coat nicely and serve.

8) Popcorn with White chocolate &Cinnamon

Preparation Time: 15 minutes
Cooking Time: 35 minutes
Ready In: 50 minutes
Servings: 4 cups

INGREDIENTS:

1/2 cup unsalted corn kernels
3 squares of almond bark or any other white-chocolate
1 cup brown sugar
1 cup pecans, roughly chopped
3/4 teaspoon cinnamon
1 teaspoon vanilla extract
1/4 cup Karo syrup or honey
1/2 teaspoon baking soda
1/2cup butter

DIRECTIONS:

1.
Pop the corn in microwave or in a deep pan coated with butter/vegetable oil over heat (do not use olive oil for popping the corn). The pan should be covered with a lid and remove the pan from stove only when popping slows down or pan is full. Remove any un-popped kernels.

2.
In a large bowl that can be place in the microwave, combine the cinnamon and brown sugar.

3.
Cut butter into small chunks and add to the sugar mixture. Also, pour the corn syrup or honey on this mixture.

4.

Microwave this mix on high heat for about 30 seconds only enough to make the butter melt. When butter melts, stir the ingredients to combine nicely. Microwave for another 4 minutes after mixing. Take out after every 2 minutes to stir.

5.
Now remove the mixture from the microwave and add in the vanilla extract and baking soda.

6.
In a large serving bowl, combine the popcorn and the chopped pecans.

7.
Pour the prepared mixture over the popcorn and pecans and mix to coat nicely.

8.
Spread the coated popcorn on a baking dish coated with cooking spray and bake in a preheated oven at 250 degrees for 30 minutes. Stir after every 10 minutes.

9.
After 30 minutes, break out a small chunk of the baked popcorn and let it cool. Taste it to make sure it is crunchy enough. If not, bake for another 5 minutes.

10.
Remove from oven and stir it one last time. Now let the popcorn cool for some time.

11.
Meanwhile, melt the almond bark or white chocolate in the microwave.

12.
Use a fork to drizzle the melted white chocolate or almond bark on the popcorn. When it cools down it will harden and stick to the popcorn. Break into chunks and enjoy!

9) Popcorn Balls with Maple Syrup&Cranberries

Preparation Time: 20 minutes
Cooking Time: 5 minutes
Ready In: 35 minutes
Servings: 12 – 15 balls

INGREDIENTS:

1 cup unsalted corn kernels
1/2 cup maple syrup
1 cup dried cranberries
1/2 cup brown sugar
3tablespoons butter

DIRECTIONS:

1.
Pop the corn in microwave or in a deep pan coated with butter/vegetable oil over heat (do not use olive oil for popping the corn) The pan should be covered with a lid and remove the pan from stove only when popping slows down or pan is full. Remove any un-popped kernels.

2.
In a small pan, mix the maple syrup and brownsugar. To this add the butter and place the pan on medium heat.

3.
Cook until the butter melts and the mixture come to a boil. Stir frequently. After about 4 minutes, the mixture will start to thicken slightly. Remove from heat.

4.
In a serving bowl combine the popcorn and dried cranberries.

5.
Pour the maple syrup mixture over the popcorn and cranberries mixtures and mix to coat evenly. Let it sit for some time to cool slightly.

6.

With moist cold hands shape the cooled popcorn mixture into small balls pressing firmly to hold the shape.

7.

Place the balls on a tray lined with wax-paper and let them sit overnight for complete cooling and hardening. Enjoy next day!

10) Popcorn with Gelatin

Preparation Time: 20 minutes
Cooking Time: 5 minutes
Ready In: 35 minutes
Servings: 12 – 15 balls

1 cup unsalted corn kernels
1 tablespoon corn syrup
1 package fruit flavoured Jell-O mix
3/4 cup sugar
1cup butter
3 tablespoons water

1.
Pop the corn in microwave or in a deep pan coated with butter/vegetable oil over heat (do not use olive oil for popping the corn). The pan should be covered with a lid and remove the pan from stove only when popping slows down or pan is full. Remove any un-popped kernels.

2.
Apply butter generously in a heavy saucepan and place it over medium heat. To this add the gelatin, corn syrup, sugar and water and heat upto 250 degree F (120 degree C). You can be sure that this temperature has reached when a small amount of the mixture on dropping into cold water forms a rigid ball.

3.
Grease a baking dish and preheat the oven to 300 degrees F (150 degrees C).

4.
Spread the popcorn over this dish and pour the prepared syrup over them. Combine to coat evenly. Place the dish in the oven and bake for 10 minutes stirring after every 5 minutes.

5.

When done, take the popcorn out of the oven and let them cool. Break into pieces or let them cool enough to form balls. Store for use later or enjoy instantly.

11) Popcorn with Sugar and Spice

Preparation Time: 25 – 27 minutes
Cooking Time: 2 – 3 minutes
Ready In: 30 minutes
Servings: 8 cups

INGREDIENTS:

1 cup unsalted corn kernels
1 teaspoon cinnamon, ground
1/4 cup sugar
2 tablespoons butter
1 tablespoon water
Salt as per taste

DIRECTIONS:

1.
Pop the corn in microwave or in a deep pan coated with butter/vegetable oil over heat (do not use olive oil for popping the corn). The pan should be covered with a lid and remove the pan from stove only when popping slows down or pan is full. Remove any un-popped kernels.

2.
Place a small pan over medium heat and add the butter to it for melting. When butter starts to melt, add the sugar, water, ground cinnamon and salt. Keep stirring till the sugar dissolves completely. Remove from heat and let it cool for some time.

3.
Meanwhile, grease a baking dish and spread the popcorn on it.

4.
Pour the mixture on the popcorn and combine to coat evenly. Now place this dish in a preheated oven at 250 degrees F and bake for 20 minutes. Stir after every 10 minutes. Enjoy warm!

12) Popcorn with Poppy seeds& Lemon

Preparation Time: 5minutes
Cooking Time: 5minutes
Ready In: 10 minutes
Servings: 2 cups

INGREDIENTS:

1/4 cup unsalted corn kernels
2 tablespoons lemon juice
Zest from 1 lemon
1 tablespoon poppy seeds
1 – 2 tablespoons coconut sugar
1 tablespoon olive oil
Salt as per taste

DIRECTIONS:

1.
Pop the corn in microwave or in a deep pan coated with butter/vegetable oil over heat (do not use olive oil for popping the corn). The pan should be covered with a lid and remove the pan from stove only when popping slows down or pan is full. Remove any un-popped kernels.

2.
In a small bowl mix the sugar, lemon juice, oil and lemon zest to combine nicely. Place the popcorn in a serving bowl and pour this mixture on them. Toss to coat evenly.

3.
Sprinkle the poppy seeds on the popcorn and toss lightly. Serve!

13) Popcorn Truffles with Coconut, Chocolate& Ginger

Preparation Time: 20minutes
Cooking Time: 15minutes
Ready In: 35 minutes
Servings: about 30 small balls

INGREDIENTS:

1/3 cup unsalted corn kernels
3 tablespoons candied ginger, minced
1 tablespoon coconut oil
2 cups mini marshmallows
1/2 coconut, shredded
1 teaspoon butter
4 ounces semi-sweet chocolate

DIRECTIONS:

1.
Pop the corn in microwave or in a deep pan coated with butter/vegetable oil over heat (do not use olive oil for popping the corn). The pan should be covered with a lid and remove the pan from stove only when popping slows down or pan is full. Remove any un-popped kernels.

2.
In a medium sized pan over low-medium heat, place the butter and marshmallows. Stir until melted and when done, remove from heat.

3.
To this add the shredded coconut and candied ginger and mix nicely.

4.
Place popcorn in a large bowl and pour the coconut mixture on it and toss to coat nicely.

5.
Spray cooking spray on your hands and start making small balls with this popcorn and coconut mixture. Keep the ready balls on a tray lined with parchment paper.

6.

Take a separate small microwave save bowl and add the chocolate to it. Microwave on high for about 2 minutes or until the chocolate melts. Keep checking on it and stirring.

7.

Add a little coconut oil to this and stir to mix nicely. Pour this chocolate in a piping cone. (You can even make a piping cone at home by snipping off a tiny corner of a zipper style plastic bag).

8.

Pipe the melted chocolate on the popcorn balls and garnish with shredded coconut and candied ginger.

9.

Place the truffles in a cool place until the chocolate is set. Enjoy!

14)Popcorn with Apple Chips &Caramel

Preparation Time: 5minutes
Cooking Time: 50minutes
Ready In: 55 minutes
Servings: 8 cups

INGREDIENTS:

1 cup unsalted corn kernels
2 (2.5 ounces) apple chips bags
1/2cup butter
1 cupbrown sugar
1 (14 ounce) can of sweetened condensed milk
1 cup corn syrup
1 teaspoon salt

DIRECTIONS:

1.
Pop the corn in microwave or in a deep pan coated with butter/vegetable oil over heat (do not use olive oil for popping the corn) The pan should be covered with a lid and remove the pan from stove only when popping slows down or pan is full. Remove any un-popped kernels.

2.
Mix the apple chips with the popcorn in a large bowl.

3.
Preheat your oven to 250 degrees and line a baking sheet with parchment paper.

4.
In a medium sized pan over medium heat, melt the butter along with the brown sugar, corn syrup and salt. Keep stirring until the mixture comes to boil.

5.
When the mixture starts to boil, pour in the condensed milk and stir continuously for 5 minutes to mix and avoid burning.

6.

Remove from the heat and pour this mixture over the popcorn and apple mix. Toss to coat evenly.

7.
Spread the mixture on the baking sheet and bake in the oven for 40 – 45 minutes. Stir after every 10 minutes.

8.
Remove from the oven and allow the popcorn to cool. When cooled, break into small pieces and enjoy!

15)Popcornwith Chocolate Chips, Cookies &Biscoff

Preparation Time: 2 – 3 minutes
Cooking Time: 5 – 7 minutes
Ready In: 10 minutes
Servings: 8 cups

INGREDIENTS:

1 cup unsalted corn kernels
1/4 cup Biscoff
1 tablespoon oil
1 cup butter cookies, crushed
1bag white chocolate chips

DIRECTIONS:

1.
Pop the corn in microwave or in a deep pan coated with butter/vegetable oil over heat (do not use olive oil for popping the corn). The pan should be covered with a lid and remove the pan from stove only when popping slows down or pan is full. Remove any un-popped kernels.

2.
In a medium sized microwave bowl combine the oil and white chocolate chips and microwave them for about 40 – 45 seconds. Stir once and microware again until the chocolate is melted and mixture becomes smooth.

3.
Now add the biscoff to this and mix nicely.

4.
Mix the popcorn and crushed cookies in a separate bowl and pour the biscoff mixture on them. Toss to coat evenly.

5.
Spread the coated popcorn on a wax paper lined tray and let it cool. When it cools the chocolate will harden. Break into pieces and store for later or serve instantly!

16)Popcorn with Nachos& Cheese

Preparation Time: 5minutes
Cooking Time: 10minutes
Ready In: 15 minutes
Servings: 12 cups

INGREDIENTS:

1 1/2 cup unsalted corn kernels
1/2 teaspoon red pepper, crushed
6 tablespoons Parmesan cheese, grated
5 tablespoons butter
1teaspoon paprika
1/2 teaspoon cumin, ground

DIRECTIONS:

1.
Pop the corn in microwave or in a deep pan coated with butter/vegetable oil over heat (do not use olive oil for popping the corn). The pan should be covered with a lid and remove the pan from stove only when popping slows down or pan is full. Remove any un-popped kernels.

2.
In a small pan melt the butter and add the cumin, paprika and red pepper to it and stir. After the butter melts, remove the pan from the heat and let it cool for some time.

3.
Place the popcorn in a serving bowl and pour this mixture on the popcorn.

4.
Sprinkle the cheese on the popcorn and toss to mix everything nicely. Serve!

17)Popcorn with Whole Nuts

Preparation Time: 10minutes
Cooking Time: 10 minutes
Ready In: 20 minutes
Servings: 12 cups

INGREDIENTS:

1 cup unsalted corn kernels
1/2 cup pumpkin seeds
1teaspoon cinnamon
2 cups pecan halves
1 cup light corn syrup
1 cup whole almonds, unblanched
1/2 cup butter
1 tablespoon chilli powder
1 1/2 cups sugar
1 teaspoon vanilla

DIRECTIONS:

1.
Pop the corn in microwave or in a deep pan coated with butter/vegetable oil over heat (do not use olive oil for popping the corn). The pan should be covered with a lid and remove the pan from stove only when popping slows down or pan is full. Remove any un-popped kernels.

2.
In a large bowl combine the popcorn, almonds, pumpkin seeds, pecans, cinnamon and chili powder. Mix evenly.

3.
Spread this mixture on a baking sheet and place in a preheated oven at 250 degrees F to warm.

4.
Side-by-side, melt the butter in a medium sized pan over medium heat and add the sugar and corn syrup to it. Stir only once lightly and then let it boil without stirring. Heat

it till the syrup turns a rich brown color. Test it by dropping a few drops in cold water. It should form stiff droplets in the water. Remove from the heat.

5.

Now add the vanilla to the butter, sugar and corn syrup mixture and stir nicely.

6.

Remove the popcorn mixture from the oven and pour this syrup over it. Toss nicely to coat evenly.

7.

Let it cool and then break into pieces. Serve!

18)Popcorn with Paprika&Almonds

Preparation Time: 10 minutes
Cooking Time: 5minutes
Ready In: 15 minutes
Servings: 8 cups

INGREDIENTS:

1/2 cup unsalted corn kernels
1teaspoon pimentd'Espelette or Hungarian hot paprika, divided
3/4 cup whole Marcona almonds, roasted
6 tablespoons unsalted butter
1/4 cup peanut oil
1 teaspoon salt, divided

DIRECTIONS:

1.
In a small bowl mix half of the paprika and half of the salt and keep aside.

2.
In a small pan over medium heat, melt the butter and remove from heat once the butter is melted. To this add the remaining paprika and salt.

3.
Pop the corn in a deep pan coated with peanut oil over heat. The pan should be covered with a lid and remove the pan from stove only when popping slows down or pan is full. Keep stirring when possible so as to evenly coat the kernels with peanut oil. Remove any un-popped kernels.

4.
Immediately add the Marcona almonds and melted butter mixture to the popcorn and cover the pan with the lid.

5.
Use oven mittens to hold the pot from both side along with the lid and shake until the almonds and popcorn are mixed well and are coated nicely with the butter mixture.

6.

Transfer to serving bowl and sprinkle the paprika and salt mixture set aside in step 1.

19)Popcorn with Crushed Peppermint &White Chocolate

Preparation Time: 5 – 7 minutes
Cooking Time: 5minutes
Ready In: 10 – 12 minutes
Servings: 4 cups

INGREDIENTS:

1/2 cup unsalted corn kernels
1/2 – 3/4 cup peppermint candies
16 ounces white chocolate chips
1 1/2 teaspoon kosher salt

DIRECTIONS:

1.
Pop the corn in microwave or in a deep pan coated with butter/vegetable oil over heat (do not use olive oil for popping the corn). The pan should be covered with a lid and remove the pan from stove only when popping slows down or pan is full. Remove any un-popped kernels.

2.
Grind the peppermint candies in a food processor finely.

3.
Place the white chocolate in a microwave safe bowl and melt in the microwave. Stir after every 30 seconds until it becomes smooth. Remove from the microwave.

4.
Mix half of the ground peppermint to the melted white chocolate.

5.
Place the popcorn in a large serving bowl and pour the white chocolate and peppermint mixture on them. Mix well to coat nicely.

6.

Sprinkle the remaining ground peppermint on the coated popcorn and spread the ready popcorn on a wax-paper lined tray.

7.

Allow the chocolate to harden and stick to the popcorn. When done, break into pieces and enjoy!

20)Popcorn with Bacon& Caramel

Preparation Time: 10minutes
Cooking Time: 30 – 35 minutes
Ready In: 40 – 45 minutes
Servings: 4 cups

INGREDIENTS:

1/2 cup unsalted corn kernels
7 pieces bacon, cooked crispy and chopped
2 tablespoons maple syrup
1/4 teaspoon paprika
1 black tea bag
1/4 cup heavy whipping cream (+1 tablespoon more)
1/2 cup peanuts
1 teaspoon salt
1 1/2 cups sugar
1/4 cup water

DIRECTIONS:

1.
Pop the corn in microwave or in a deep pan coated with butter/vegetable oil over heat
(do not use olive oil for popping the corn). The pan should be covered with a lid and
remove the pan from stove only when popping slows down or pan is full. Remove any
un-popped kernels.

2.
In a medium sized pan over medium heat add the cream for boiling. Also add the tea
bag. Bring cream to a nice boil (do not over boil) and remove the pan from heat. Let it sit
while the tea gives the cream its rich flavor. Occasionally press the tea bag with the
back of a spoon to release flavor. Discard the tea bag.

3.
Spread the popcorn on a baking tray lined with baking paper. Sprinkle salt on the
popcorn and toss to coat.

4.
Sprinkle bacon and peanuts on top of the popcorn. Preheat the oven to 150 degree C.

5.

In a large pan over medium heat, combine the sugar and maple syrup. Heat till the sugar dissolves. Then increase the heat and bring the syrup to a boil without stirring. Continue till the syrup turns to deep amber color.

6.

Remove the syrup from heat and immediately add the cream. This will cause the mixture to bubble up, it's normal. Stir until blended.

7.

Pour this mix over the popcorn and toss to coat evenly. Now place this tray in the oven and bake until the caramel coats the popcorn evenly and becomes shiny. This should take about 20 minutes. Stir once or twice.

8.

Remove from oven and let the popcorn cool completely. Toss once or twice to make sure they have completely cooled.

9.

Break into pieces and store for later or enjoy instantly!

21)Popcorn Balls with Vanilla &Peanut Butter

Preparation Time: 20minutes
Cooking Time: 10minutes
Ready In: 4 hours and 30 minutes (includes time for balls to harden, i.e, 2 – 4 hours)
Servings: 15 – 20 balls

INGREDIENTS:

2/3 cups lightly salted corn kernels
2/3 cup granulated sugar
2 tablespoons honey
1 ½ cups dry roasted peanuts, roughly chopped
2 teaspoons vanilla extract
¼ cup Reese's Peanut Butter Chips
2/3 cup smooth peanut butter
2/3 cup light corn syrup

DIRECTIONS:

1.
Pop the corn in microwave or in a deep pan coated with butter/vegetable oil over heat (do not use olive oil for popping the corn). The pan should be covered with a lid and remove the pan from stove only when popping slows down or pan is full. Remove any un-popped kernels.

2.
In a small saucepan over medium heat, combine the corn syrup and sugar and bring to boil. Test it by dropping a few drops in cold water. It should form stiff droplets in the water. If not, heat it for some more time. Remove from the heat.

3.
Now add the honey, vanilla and peanut butter to this mixture and stir nicely.

4.
In a separate bowl combine the popcorn and peanut butter chips.

5.

Pour the corn syrup mixture over the popcorn and toss to coat evenly. Let it sit for some time to cool slightly.

7.
Once the mixture is cool enough to handle, lightly grease your hands and start forming small balls.

8.
Place the balls on a parchment paper lined tray and keep aside for 2 – 4 hours. Serve!

22)Healthy Popcorn Salad

Preparation Time: 10 minutes
Cooking Time: 5minutes
Ready In: 15 minutes
Servings: 10 – 12 cups

INGREDIENTS:

2/3 cups unsalted corn kernels
1-1/4 cups cheddar cheese, shredded and divided
3/4 cup mayonnaise
1 can (8 ounces) sliced water chestnuts, drained
2 tablespoons minced chives
1 cup diced celery
1/4 cup shredded carrot
3/4 cup crumbled cooked bacon, divided
Salt as per taste

DIRECTIONS:

1.
Pop the corn in microwave or in a deep pan coated with butter/vegetable oil over heat (do not use olive oil for popping the corn). The pan should be covered with a lid and remove the pan from stove only when popping slows down or pan is full. Remove any un-popped kernels.

2.
Combine the mayo, cheese, chestnuts, celery, carrots, 1/2 cup bacon and chives in a large bowl and mix well.

3.
To this add the popcorn and mix nicely. Sprinkle a little salt and mix again.

4.
Spread this mixture into a lettuce lined serving bowl and top with the remaining bacon and cheese. Serve!

23)Popcorn with M & M's &Marshmallow

Preparation Time: 5minutes
Cooking Time: 10minutes
Ready In: 15 minutes
Servings: 16 cups

INGREDIENTS:

2 cups unsalted corn kernels
1 lb. package mini marshmallows
1/2 cup butter
1 cup M & M's

DIRECTIONS:

1.
Pop the corn in microwave or in a deep pan coated with butter/vegetable oil over heat (do not use olive oil for popping the corn). The pan should be covered with a lid and remove the pan from stove only when popping slows down or pan is full. Remove any un-popped kernels.

2.
Melt butter in a small pan over medium heat. Add the marshmallows to this and stir. Heat till melted.

3.
Pour this over the popcorn and toss well to coat evenly.

4.
Add the M & M's and toss again. Serve!

24)Popcorn with Spiced Nuts&Blue Cheese

Preparation Time: 10minutes
Cooking Time: 20minutes
Ready In: 30 minutes
Servings: 18 – 20 cups

INGREDIENTS:

3/4 cup popcorn kernels
1/2 cup almonds, coarsely chopped
2 tablespoons heavy cream
1/8 teaspoon ground cloves
1/2 cup roasted unsalted peanuts, coarsely chopped
2 cups sugar
11/2 teaspoons freshly grated nutmeg
3/4 teaspoon ground cinnamon
1/4 teaspoon ground cardamom
3 tablespoons vegetable oil
Finely grated zest of 1/2 orange
1/4 cup water
Seeds scraped from 1 split vanilla bean
1/2 tablespoon kosher salt
1 teaspoon black pepper,freshly ground
Great Hill Blue cheese, for serving

DIRECTIONS:

1.
Pop the corn in microwave or in a deep pan coated with butter/vegetable oil over heat
(do not use olive oil for popping the corn). The pan should be covered with a lid and
remove the pan from stove only when popping slows down or pan is full. Remove any
un-popped kernels.

2.
Preheat the oven to 325 degrees F and spread the almonds and peanuts on a baking
tray. Toast these in the oven lightly for about 6 minutes. Stir them at least once to
prevent from burning. Remove from oven and keep aside.

3.

In a large pan over high heat, boil the water and add sugar to it. Heat until sugar dissolves completely and the syrup starts to bubble and reaches golden color.

4.

Now add in the cream. Be careful as the syrup may sputter. Stir continuously while adding the cream.

5.

Remove from the heat and add the vanilla, cinnamon, lemon zest, cardamom, cloves, nutmeg, salt and pepper and mix nicely.

6.

Now start adding the popcorn and roasted nuts into this mixture and keep stirring with a wooden spoon until all the popcorn and nuts are well coated. Keep your hands quick not allowing the caramel to harden up.

7.

Spread the coated popcorn and nuts on a large baking sheet lined with parchment paper and allow them to cool completely. Once cooled, arrange in a serving bowl and garnish with blue cheese. Serve!

25)Popcorn with White Chocolate & Assorted Sprinkles

Preparation Time: 5 minutes
Cooking Time: 10 minutes
Ready In: 15 minutes
Servings: 6 cups

INGREDIENTS:

2/3 cupunsalted corn kernels
1 cup cake batter mix
1 1/2 cups almond or white chocolate
1/4 cup vegetable shortening
Assorted sprinkles

DIRECTIONS:

1.
Pop the corn in microwave or in a deep pan coated with butter/vegetable oil over heat (do not use olive oil for popping the corn). The pan should be covered with a lid and remove the pan from stove only when popping slows down or pan is full. Remove any un-popped kernels.

2.
But the white chocolate or almond bark in a microwave safe bowl and heat in the microwave until chocolate is fully melted. Stir occasionally.

3.
Add the vegetable shortening to this melted chocolate and stir until everything melts and becomes smooth in consistency. You can re-heat the mixture by heating again in the microwave if required.

4.
Now add the cake mix to this and mix nicely. Preferably whisk using a light hand whisker.

5.
Pour this mixture over the popcorn arranged on a large tray and toss to coat evenly.

6.

Sprinkle immediately with assorted sprinkles of your choice and let them sit to cool and harden.

7.

Once hardened, take out in a serving bowl and enjoy!

26)Popcorn with Milky Way chocolate

Preparation Time: 5 minutes
Cooking Time: 15minutes
Ready In: 20 minutes
Servings: 4 cups

INGREDIENTS:

1/2 cupunsalted corn kernels
10 fun size Milky Way candy bars, chopped
6 ounces chocolate chips
3 tablespoons half and half
4 ounces caramels, unwrapped

DIRECTIONS:

1.
Pop the corn in microwave or in a deep pan coated with butter/vegetable oil over heat (do not use olive oil for popping the corn). The pan should be covered with a lid and remove the pan from stove only when popping slows down or pan is full. Remove any un-popped kernels.

2.
In a small microwave safe bowl place the chocolate chips and heat them in the microwave until completely melted. Stir to check.

3.
Similarly melt the caramels and add in the half and half mixing and melting till they form a smooth mix.

4.
Spread the popcorn on a large baking sheet and pour the melted chocolate on them. Toss to coat evenly.

5.
Now add the candy pieces to the popcorn and toss again.

6.

Pour the melted caramel over this and toss gently. Let it sit for a couple of hours to harden. Serve!

27)Popcorn with Yummy Yogurt

Preparation Time: 5minutes
Cooking Time: 10minutes
Ready In: 15 minutes
Servings: 4 cups

INGREDIENTS:

1/2 cupunsalted corn kernels
1/3 cup light corn syrup
1 cup plain yogurt
1 cup brown sugar

DIRECTIONS:

1.
Pop the corn in microwave or in a deep pan coated with butter/vegetable oil over heat (do not use olive oil for popping the corn). The pan should be covered with a lid and remove the pan from stove only when popping slows down or pan is full. Remove any un-popped kernels.

2.
In a large pan over medium heat combine the corn syrup, yogurt and brown sugar. Cook until the mix reaches hard ball stage (Test it by dropping a few drops in cold water. It should form stiff droplets in the water. If not, heat it for some more time).

3.
Pour this mix over the popcorn and toss to coat evenly. Serve!

28)Popcorn with Pumpkin Pie spice

Preparation Time: 5minutes
Cooking Time: 1 hour and 10 minutes (includes baking time)
Ready In: 1 hour and 15 minutes
Servings: 10 cups

INGREDIENTS:

1 1/3 cups salted corn kernels
1 1/2 teaspoons pumpkin pie spice
1/4 cup light corn syrup
1 cup packed brown sugar
6 tablespoons butter
1/2 teaspoon baking soda
Salt as per taste
Cooking spray

DIRECTIONS:

1.
Pop the corn in microwave or in a deep pan coated with butter/vegetable oil over heat (do not use olive oil for popping the corn). The pan should be covered with a lid and remove the pan from stove only when popping slows down or pan is full. Remove any un-popped kernels.

2.
Coat a large mixing bowl with cooking spray and take out the popcorn in it. Preheat the oven to 250 degree F and line a baking sheet with parchment paper.

3.
In a medium sized over medium-high heat, pour the corn syrup and add the butter, salt, pepper and brown sugar. Mix everything nicely and bring to a boil, stirring frequently.

4.
Remove from heat and immediately add the baking soda and pumpkin spice and mix nicely.

5.
Pour this hot caramel over the popcorn and toss to coat the popcorn evenly.

6.
Transfer this mix to the baking sheet and bake for 1 hour stirring the popcorn after every 20 minutes.

7.
When done, remove from the oven and allow the popcorn to cool. Then, gently break into pieces and serve!

29)Popcorn Treats with Apricots &dried Cherries

Preparation Time: 10minutes
Cooking Time: 10 minutes
Ready In: 20 minutes
Servings: 10 cups

INGREDIENTS:

1 1/3 cups unsalted corn kernels
1/2 cup sugar-free apricot preserves
1/4 cup light corn syrup
1/2 teaspoon lemon juice
3/4 cup dried cherries
3/4 cup sugar
1/2 cup + 2 tablespoons water
Cooking spray

DIRECTIONS:

1.
Pop the corn in microwave or in a deep pan coated with butter/vegetable oil over heat (do not use olive oil for popping the corn). The pan should be covered with a lid and remove the pan from stove only when popping slows down or pan is full. Remove any un-popped kernels.

2.
In a small pan over medium heat combine the water, apricot preserves, sugar, corn syrup and lemon juice. Bring this mix to a boil stirring continuously until sugar dissolves completely. Cook until the mixture is of a thick consistency which forms ropes when dripping from a spoon.

3.
In a serving bowl mix the popcorn and cherries. Pour the syrup over these and toss to coat evenly.

4.

Spray a deep baking dish with cooking spray and spread the popcorn mixture over it. Press it from the top to blow out any air. Let it sit like this to cool down completely.

5.
When cooled, cut into squares and serve!

30)Popcorn with Mint&Fudge Cookie

Preparation Time: 10 minutes
Cooking Time: 10 minutes
Ready In: 20 minutes
Servings: 10 cups

INGREDIENTS:

1 cupunsalted corn kernels
1 1/2 cups white chocolate chips
1 1/2 cups fudge mint cookies, chopped & divided
3/4 cup chocolate candies, divided
1 cup miniature marshmallows
1 teaspoon shortening
1/4 cup green candy melts
3 tablespoon sprinkles

DIRECTIONS:

1.
Pop the corn in microwave or in a deep pan coated with butter/vegetable oil over heat (do not use olive oil for popping the corn). The pan should be covered with a lid and remove the pan from stove only when popping slows down or pan is full. Remove any un-popped kernels.

2.
Crush 1/2 cup cookies to form fine crumbs and keep aside with 1/4 cup chocolate candies.

3.
In a large bowl mix the marshmallows, popcorn, 1 cup fudge mint cookie pieces and the remaining 1/2 cup chocolate candies.

4.
In a microwave safe bowl place the white chocolate chips and shortening and heat until melted completely stirring every 30 seconds.

5.

Pour this over the popcorn mixture and toss to coat evenly. Sprinkle the crushed cookies and candies set aside in step 2 on top of this mixture.

6.
In a separate microwave safe bowl melt the green candy melts. Pour this into a piping cone. (You can make a piping cone at home by snipping off a tiny corner of a zipper plastic bag.

7.
Pipe the melted green candy melt over the popcorn and garnish with the sprinkles. Enjoy!

31)Popcorn with Pecan Cake

Preparation Time: 10 minutes
Cooking Time: 15minutes
Ready In: 25 minutes
Servings: 2 cups

INGREDIENTS:

1/4 cup popcorn kernels
8 ounces white candy melts
1 cup pecans
2 tablespoons butter
3 tablespoons sugar
1/2 cup butter pecan cake mix
Salt as per taste

DIRECTIONS:

1.
Pop the corn in microwave or in a deep pan coated with butter/vegetable oil over heat (do not use olive oil for popping the corn). The pan should be covered with a lid and remove the pan from stove only when popping slows down or pan is full. Remove any un-popped kernels.

2.
Toast the pecans in a frying pan over low heat, stirring often, just until you smell them.

3.
Melt butter in a small pan over medium heat and add the sugar to it. Heat and stir until the butter melts completely and sugar dissolves fully.

4.
Remove from heat and add salt and stir. Immediately pour this mix over the popcorn and toss to coat evenly.

5.
In a separate pan over medium heat melt the candy melts. Add the cake mix in this and stir well to combine finely.

6.

Pour this mix over the popcorn. Also add the toasted pecans to the popcorn and toss to coat everything evenly.

7. Spread out the ready popcorn on a large baking sheet lined with wax-paper and lit it cool until the candy hardens. When done, store for use later or enjoy instantly!

Printed in Great Britain
by Amazon